RHYTHMS OF LIFE:

AN ANTHOLOGY OF MODERN POETRY

ROSELLE THOMPSON

EAGLE PUBLICATIONS

Published by Eagle Publications
P O Box 73374, London W3 3FZ, England.

A Paperback Original

First published in the United Kingdom in 2019

Text copyright © 2019 Roselle Thompson

The right of Roselle Thompson to be identified as the Author
of this work has been asserted by her.

ISBN: 978-0-9542325-0-4

A CIP catalogue record for this book is available from the British Library

All Rights Reserved.
This book is sold subject to the condition that it
shall not, by way of trade or otherwise, be lent, hired out or otherwise
circulated in any form of binding or cover other than that in which it is
published. No part of this publication may be reproduced, stored in
a retrieval system, or transmitted in any form or by any means
(electronic, mechanical, photocopying, recording or otherwise)
without the prior written permission of Eagle Publications.

All paper used by Eagle Publications is SFI (Sustainable Forestry Initiative)
and PEFC (Programme for the Endorsement of Forest
Certification Schemes) Certified.

This is a work of fiction. Names, characters, incidents and dialogues
are products of the author's imagination or are used fictitiously.
Any resemblance to actual people, living or dead, events or
locales is entirely coincidental.

Printed in the United Kingdom and United States by
Lightning Source for Eagle Publishers

www.eaglepublications.co.uk

CONTENTS

London	1
Have you ever?	3
Ivan's War	5
Ode to the Thames	6
Angel	7
Childhood	8
Brexit Divorce	9
Driving Home	10
Don't Cry For Me!	11
Eating a Julie Mango	13
Rain	14
A Black Mother to Her Son	15
Falling Down	18
Friday Night - Youth Anthem	19
Ode to Seasons in the Tropics	20
Spring	21
My Grandmother's Hands	22
Grenville Market	23
I Quit!	25
I'll Dance at Your Wedding	26
In the Castle of my Hoodie	27
Island Girl	28
La Bay	30
Letting Go	31
Mad Woman:Fact or Fiction?	32
Mum on a City Bus	34
My Teacher	36
Are They Misfits?	37
Her Smile	38
Oh My Soul!	39
Old Age Romance	41
Out of the Mouths of Babes	42
Maud's Second Time Around	44
Miracle of Friendship	46
Seasons	47
The Storm	48

Valentine	49
What About Us?	50
Woman of Destiny!	51
Down, But Not Out!	52
Kaiso Farewell Rhythms!	53
Equality	55
Conversations in Rhythms	56
I Will Keep Rising	57
National Mentality	58
Dancing with Stars	59
Diaspora Blues	60
Who is he?	61
I aint no snitch!	62
Goodbye!	64
GLOSSARY	**65**

INTRODUCTION

Rhythms of Life: An Anthology of Modern Poetry is an intriguing collection of poems that take you on a spirited, poetic journey; exploring different experiences via a variety of perspectives, moods, personas and everyday moments, in ways that reflect rhythmical periods in our lives. Each poem has its natural cadence, flowing like a provocative bird of paradise, and as a compilation, they present a variety of rhythms through different voices and emotions which show a fusion; on both the personal and naturist level. The poems explore human conditions, which can be seen through subject matters that range from; childhood, time, old age, seasons, memory, love, war, wisdom, the heart, the inevitability of death, politics, patriotism, youth and a double allegiance to both Grenada, (where I was born), and England. Therefore, from these myriad perspectives, the Anthology, which shows the relationship of humanity to nature, is both appealing and thought-provoking.

For example, in ***Rhythms of Life***, even the simple passage of time can be seen as malign and the poem entitled, **Who is He?** suggests that at times humanity seems to be under the control of an external force which conspires against us. This idea is also emphasised in the poem ***Ivan's War***, where Hurricane Ivan (2004), is presented in military terms; as nature at war with

Grenadians, in ways that show their vulnerability and powerlessness against hurricane destructions.

There is also repeated emphasis on the healing power of nature which pervades organic nature, in ways that suggest human life is full of perpetual renewals; seen in its juxtaposition with seasonal cycles. However, the natural environment can be made more complex by social circumstances; as is seen in the poem London. This poem shows how the landscape is embroiled in socially degraded activities on streets, evidenced by the predatory nature of youths with guns and knives. In it, the past World Wars are compared with London's present social environment, its communities and our general attitude to youth crimes.

However, the poems can also bring sunshine to your day, such as in **Eating a Julie Mango**, which highlights how memory plays its part in recalling the pleasurable and sensuous way of eating a Julie Mango: whilst others in the Anthology such as **Ode to the Thames; Brexit; In the Castle of My Hoodie; Don't Cry for Me!** and **A Black Mother to her Son,** are sobering; seen from reflective, political and contemplative perspectives.

In general, hearing the words "rhythms of life," may bring to mind the idea of movement; such as dancing, music, or timing, to the perfect co-ordination of beats or sounds. To an extent, this is true because such associative movements also relate to our personal sense of rhythm or balance. But in the context of this Anthology, I have explored through the poems, how our human interactions relate to nature's own rhythms or particular times, in our cycle of life on Planet Earth.

The most quoted view on how our lives relate to rhythms or to notable times, has been expressed by King Solomon, in one of the simplest statements that seems to give a universal definition, is as follows: **"To everything there is a season, a time for every purpose under heaven:"** He then clarified his statement by breaking down its meaning into rhythmical periods in our lives: *"a time for every purpose under heaven: a time to be born, and a time to die; a time to plant, and a time to pluck up what is planted; a time to kill, and a time to heal; a time to break down, and a time to build up; a time to weep, and a time to laugh; a time to mourn, and a time to dance; a time to cast away stones, and a time to gather stones; a time to embrace, and a time to refrain from embracing; a time to gain, and a time to lose; a time to keep, and a time to throw away; a time to tear, and a time to sew; a time to keep silence, and a time to speak; a time to love, and a time to hate; a time of war, and a time of peace, (Eccl:3:1-8)."*

However, despite its religious source of origin, these words also resonate globally to human activities in our existence. For example, we have stages in our lives that are good times and bad times; times when we are in control of our lives or things around us, and there are other times when this is not the case; reflecting King Solomon's *"times"* or *"seasons."* Therefore, in pondering the marvels of life, we realise that there is a rhythm to everything around us: in our choice of colours, in our feelings, in our environment, in our names, and in our association with things around us, in our interaction with people and more. These interactions tend to have an impact on us as individuals, as well as on our relationship groups; from the moment we are born, to the time that we die.

So in suggesting that our lives and everything around us are embodied in nature-driven rhythms, we can also find new ways of expressing or interpreting them. This is especially so because certain rhythms can be intertwined and therefore present a symbiotic balance between the intellectual or institutional periphery, and the personal appreciation of the intense feelings, which these rhythms evoke in our lives.

Therefore, in this Anthology, I present the **"Rhythms of Life"** as it reflects synchronicity, individuality, and rhythmical oneness in our universe and in the way we see and do everyday things; in order for the reader to experience pleasure via an understanding and appreciation of poetry.

Another reason for writing this Poetry Anthology, has been influenced by my 27 years of teaching, especially to 15 and 16 year old students (Years 10 & 11); nearing the end of their compulsory school education and preparing for their *GCSE exams. Their dilemma stems from having to learn, understand and critically analyse a themed cluster of 16 poems, at a time when they also have other genres to interrogate, (such as novels, plays - heritage and contemporary; as well as Shakespeare's plays), whilst preparing for their GCSEs. Their schools' strategy of leaving Poetry learning until this latter stage of their education, for a long time, has led to students persistently stating that they find poetry to be an unnecessary burden in their lives, and vow that when the exams are over, to either *"burn their exam anthologies"* or *"never want to see or read a poem again, ever!!"* In response to these drastic outpouring of negative emotions for this literary genre, I have had to reason with many, by producing an alternative strategy in order to help them become part of poetry's creative process; in other words, via a learning by doing approach to understanding poetry. My view is, by allowing students to produce their own written poems, enables them to learn how poems are formulated. Not surprisingly, the result was that they began to enjoy the sentiments expressed in the form and structure of poetic works.

As a result, this experience has led me to conclude that poetry has not been given its fair share of study-time devoted to it within the curriculum; compared with other subject areas in English Language and English Literature. The fact is, learning poetry as the students have had to do, at the end of their compulsory education, (age 16yrs); they suggested, is forcing or imposing poetry on them, as a *"have to"*, rather than a *"want to"* learning approach to poetry. The result is that students judge poetry as a hateful *"humbug,"* and as something they would not be looking at in life again.

It is my belief that a solution to this dilemma lies in both strategy and preparation time; to help students develop an appreciation for poetry, beginning from the start of Secondary school (Year 7 – age 11) and continuing with an input in each subsequent year, till the age of 16.

This would provide a multitude of benefits:
(1). Developing familiarity with the genre; (2). Creating an appreciation for poetry; (3). Fostering an understanding of the poetic form; (4). Gaining cumulative pleasure via the aesthetics of poetic expression. Ultimately, this would enable students to engage in competent, critical analysis and evaluation, which are required for the National exams at GCSE stage; 5 years later. This strategy would also prevent the kind of fear engendered by the Unseen Poems Exam component of the GCSE English Literature Paper. It would also reduce the fear and panic associated with the common-place series of *"what-if"* questions: *"What if I don't understand the poem when I read it? What if I have nothing to say in the analysis; What if I don't like the poem and don't have much to say about it?"* These psychological barriers pin-point the insecurity and loathing, with which they associate poetry: the fact that it is viewed as esoteric, cryptic, or irrelevant to their lives.

For the majority of these students, poetry will never be a part of their lives beyond the GCSE stage in their educational development, and for many, the possibility of choosing English Literature at Advanced level (A levels), is an unlikely consideration. Therefore, it is a loss to inclusion at Higher Education and beyond; as well as to the students personally - those who prefer not to engage in poetic appreciation for reasons already stated.

Therefore, in attempting to redress the imbalance during my own teaching, I introduced some of the poems included in this **"Rhythms of Life: An Anthology of Modern Poetry,"** in order to help students realise that the subject of poetry is not far removed from issues that affect their own lives. The poems were meant to show them how, if anything, poetry has everything to do with their expressions of feelings, reflections and opinions; on any given subject.

Additionally, another strategy has been to make students write their own poetry, about subjects they feel passionate about e.g. bullying, differences, politics, responsibilities and seasonal subjects; which has made their appreciation and understanding of the creative process, far more appealing. The result was that many of those who had earlier vowed to hate literature for the rest of their lives, because of its perceived lack of its connectivity, began to express an interest in the subject, in a ways that restored their faith in appreciating WORDS on a page. In fact, the students soon realised that those learnt skills, were transferrable across other subject areas in the curriculum; in a most pleasing way. Therefore, to those students who have inspired me to write, in order to inspire them; (See *Glossary sample*), I dedicate **Rhythms of Life: An Anthology of Modern Poetry**, with gratitude.

Roselle Thompson
London 2019

GCSE – General Certificate of Education (In Britain) - a public examination in specified subjects for 16-year-old schoolchildren. It replaced the GCE O level and CSE in the 1970's.

RHYTHMS OF LIFE

AN ANTHOLOGY OF MODERN POETRY

Roselle Thompson

London

Once we welcomed the West Indian Servicemen's Call,
'Come and fight for your Motherland, come one and all,
Great Britain has been lambasted, she has been smitten
By German bombers: Help us, so she will not be beaten!'
Men marched with pride in the tropical Caribbean heat,
Uniformed, to the sound of our marching band's beat;
Defiant our faces with goals and Union Jacks unfurled,
Mission: rid the [1]King of Hitler's might, so we were told.

Our islands dispatched West India Regiment[2] with glee,
Our Britain to save, so that we can all be totally free;
Our gladdened hearts reflected in the islands' pride,
Our victory is sure we believed, as in God we abide.
60 years and battle's bugle reverberates in mind today,
When Jack, John, patriotic soldiers; fell that fateful day
As we fearlessly fought alongside Empire's colonial sons;
Battling till the moment of surrender and Britain won.

But today I hear of cries of war, within a city's battle-field,
On London's rich, multi-cultured streets, so crime-filled
With youths wielding guns, knives; with terror they strike
At others with no sense of pride; surely, that is not right!
I sit and wonder when newsreels blare yet another scare;
Families losing sons on streets, without a single dam care!
Such wanton waste of precious life, so mercilessly taken
From those mourning their loss - for no apparent reason!

O nation miserable - accepting socially degrading streets,
Wake up! Save your youth and sound the social retreat;
Don't wait when it's just them and act only when it's me!
Silence silly street battle-cries and take back your authority.
Their war is raging outside, from silent festering fires inside,
But do they know of our past glory and our willing sacrifice?
Or pride in displaying the true meaning of united feelings
For a country where reasons resonated within our beings?

Return from slumber; good morals to our vibrant young lives!
Return to service; teach them of purpose, not hate or strife!
Return the hope that each dawn brings; show thankfulness!
Return pride that nurtures love and labour for a quick redress!

Notes:
[1.] The monarch before Queen Elizabeth II was King George VI (1936-1952).
[2.] See **Glossary**

Have you ever...?

Have you ever laughed so much till you wanted to cry
At a funny joke that nearly, almost, split your side?
Or wandered through the woods with feet unshod
Feeling the tickly wet, sticky, mud between your toes?
Or try to wipe them clean on soft, soggy, wet grass,
Breaking small crispy twigs under feet as you pass?

Have you ever shouted loudly among leafy green trees
And hear your voice echo, as you savour the breeze?
Have you ever thrown stones into a calm, silent lake?
Then watch them flip, skip, drop and then quietly plop!
Making ripples that ring outwards for ages and ages, or
Pick fruit from trees standing; not letting them drop?

Have you ever bathed in a cool early morning stream,
Whilst trying to piece together a forgotten dream?
Or lie awake in the warm sun, feeling its healing balm,
As your mind dance in shadows - with stress-free calm:
Have you ever skipped away among tall, lazy, bushes?
Or roll down green, grassy, hills for as long as you please.

Have you ever caught the falling rain with your tongue?
Or bathe your face in it as it pours, then jump in puddles
Whilst waiting for more; or tell yourself it doesn't matter
That your hair's all wet, you'll never really catch a cold.
Have you ever licked a melting ice-cream in a crispy cone;
As the sweet, sticky, liquid races down to your elbow?

Have you ever climbed a tree and grazed your left knee
And wait for the scab to heal, so that later you can peel?
Or claim you need a plaster as you nurse the old wound;
Then watch your brother's sullen face when you are given
All of Mum's favourite chocolates, for your painful woes;
Later you laugh, share with him and make plans for more.

Have you ever smeared winter snow-flakes on your face?
Frolicking in the powdery whiteness, making chirpy gurgles;
Or experience the petrichor of rain on very hot dry terrain?
Have you ever seen mirages rise as they sizzle and dance?
Or sip nectar from juices so sweet, in the sweltering heat;
As you prance, hands in air to mental musical beats?

Let's say when you have done these things, my friend,
You understand *how* to live!

Ivan's War

Battened down hatches, doors sealed, prayers said
For respite, safety, pity, pardon; and no one dead:
Through waiting and watching, all feeling aghast,
Hurricane bombarded ambush; like spitfire blasts.

He clobbered the strong trees, chastised our green land,
Pummelled the island, while all vowed to take a stand;
Not like old [1]*Janet*, who in '55, plummeted our house,
And made our brave, little Island, tremble like a mouse.

But [2]*Ivan* in comparison, with vengeance did strike
To wreck, raid and ruin our proud little Isle of Spice;
For hours he spewed rain like a savage, wild beast,
While sea waters blasted; winds besieging from east.

Men, women held fast; as in dug-out war trenches,
Fortifying all kinds of Grenada's hurricane defences
In defiance: to counteract and fast send *Ivan* to hell,
Never sounding the retreat; as his onslaught to quell.

And finally when over, our [3]Armistice day showed,
Ivan had destroyed our infrastructure and more;
We counted the cost, gave thanks for near-misses,
Vowed to replenish our island and pick up the pieces.

Note:
1. Hurricane Janet – **See Glossary**
2. Hurricane Ivan – **See Glossary**
3. Armistice- **See Glossary**

Ode to the Thames

She meanders in sacred silence from Estuary's head
Reflecting blessings from heaven, that she is cared;
Flowing with pride along scenic views of our city,
Snaking, she rises, tirelessly running to the Sea:
Navigating her course over forty-five ancient locks,
Resplendent, she glides around island-like rocks.
Observed by Palaces; Hampton and Westminster,
London Eye captures the path; so you can see her
Rotating, repeating; iconic gem in our biggest city,
Recording changes, thousands of years of history.
Travelling, by God-given will, with so much to do,
Teased by incandescent moons, who lovingly woo
Whilst sunlight serenades, from tributaries feed;
To provide Londoner's travelling and watery needs.
Boats cruise on her surface, so many she pleases,
Never in hurry; but Big Ben and Houses she teases.
Pregnant with secrets of London's worst and best,
Longest in England, our Thames beats all the rest;
Knows stories of lovers, Royal bliss - even some mess
Accidents: blunders, [1]Guy Fawkes and [2]Marchioness.
But see how she lights up; sites sparkle in the night,
One in a million, she's unique; oh such a pretty sight!
On banks, fireworks reflect myriad colourful hues,
As cheering crowds of thousands ring in the [3]New.
What joy seeing her photos from lovely city bridges?
All pictorial mementos to grace some global fridges!
That famous Ole River will just keep rolling along...

See Glossary:
[1] Guy Fawkes
[2] Marchioness
[3] New = New Year Celebrations

Angel

One is missing in that celestial heaven,
So perfect, peaceful and so purely given;
A sweet, sinless, baby with face all aglow,
This cherub, a wingless angel we all adore.

Unbelievable, God has so generously sent
This precious little bundle of joy that is meant
To crown our lives, this is specially beautified
With rare blessings; now we are truly satisfied.

How delicate her face, a tiny porcelain figure!
Like a fairy she breathes, so gently with ease;
Eyes clasp in angelic reverie, calmly she sleeps,
Smiling in silence; with joy, we just sit and stare!

Childhood

Screams of laughter, merriment and play-fight,
Chalking the playground in colours very bright,
Chasing, jumping, tugging, everyone's around
Your best friend; who is slumped on the ground.

Wanting to be an adult you really can't wait
To go out with friends on your very first date,
And blast favourite music as you try to imitate
Those pop stars; the idols you vow to emulate.

You wonder if life will bring envisioned pleasure,
Counting moments you will always treasure,
Impatiently waiting when all schooling will end,
Then sample expected university fashion trends.

Can't wait to join grown-ups and reach adulthood,
Thinking life would be simple; as it really should -
But stay in the moment; this time of little care,
Be satisfied with your childhood; time that is rare.

[1]Brexit Divorce

The time has come, to part the waves -
Experienced divorce - jagged hearts in pain;
Fear turn to anger, expectation to regret,
Glory to shame and confidence to despair;
Loathing, bickering; divisions multiplied,
As you shun the zest of a dauntless past,
Bowing to history's vengeful contention
You know, I've been right there before!
Can never turn the clock BACK, they say -
No, no - not now!

Bombastically burying heads in the sand,
Riotously rejecting a Union's open hands,
Infamously inviting pleas to Remain, that
Triumphantly tussle with forces to Leave,
Anxiously waiting, they learn their fate;
Indictments indicate, time to contemplate,
Now nervously recalling the blighted past,
Voices of reason, against those of dissent,
Defiantly fuse with, 'We'd like to repent!'
No, no - not now!

Taste and see our emotions nakedness;
Raw, when fused with patriotic disarray.
Complex, confused, fuzzy futures await;
As divorce clocks tick the knell of Exit-day.
For hands that held those decision pens
Long made imperative marks to withdraw;
Pull stiff upper-lips on tightly-clenched jaws.
Awake from slumber, to an imminent dawn,
Where Time beckons to a brand new day!
The milk is spilt; should you feel any guilt?
No, no - not really – not now!

[1] Brexit - **See Glossary**

Driving Home

The night road is a wet black ribbon in flight,
Divided by many long broken lines of white;
Fly by as busy wipers rise and fall, to drain
And scrape smears of slanted mizzling rain.
Cats' eyes wink and instantly disappear,
But red, orange, green lights, always there;
Yellow lamps as sentinels stand, giving light,
Blotting out darkness for my tired eye-sight;
And the radio softly soothes my jaded mind,
In helter-skelter, home-ward bound to unwind.

Don't Cry For Me!

Don't cry for me when I'm finally dead and gone,
I'll probably be dancing, celebrating with a song;
Having left a world full of pain, troubles and strife,
From ignorance; in refusing each other to embrace
Differences; as priceless wealth love could replace.
Instead, fostering a planet of hate and reckless greed,
Whilst dominating groups as the priority of his needs:
No, don't cry for me, I will happily be gone from here.

They drop bombs on others and think it's alright,
Obliterating the weak ones with their reckless might;
But will feed their loved ones, protect, and even take
From the lowly and the weak; those whom they hate;
Then instil fear to show it's them you must emulate,
So victims will yearn to be like that and gravitate
To what's projected – greed, power; seen as great!
No, don't cry for me, I'll be well away from it all.

They demand your food, buying at very little price,
But re-selling, insist on rates that always cost twice
As high; this makes you poor, so begging is a must,
So your mindset is trained for hunger, crime, or lust:
They extract your natural riches; diamonds and gold,
Exploited, you're forced to forage, hungry in the cold;
Then say that you have nothing; not even the power
To fight against rumours that your brains are smaller!
No, don't cry for me; hubristic downfall - is a must.

He preaches race-hate but quotes long religious verse,
Bamboozles the world; saying his god is good and just,
Reversing years of harmony in your neighbourhood;
And men and women argue for reasons why they should
Let guns do the talking: social media show police stalking -
Mowing down preachers, teachers, brothers, and those
Who are against misery, injustice, corruption and hate.
To instil fear of the new world order, for supremacy's sake:
No, no, don't cry for me, your own silence has said it all.

But soon they will wake up and surely must discover
That with bomb blast repercussions, they may not recover
From poisonous air, that judicious Wind equally shares
Being in the same boat; all shedding the same stinking tears;
And the goods that they stole, no value it will hold,
Nor their weapons and media, or diamonds and gold;
I only hope and pray that for little children's sake,
There's time to make amends, before it's too late:
No, don't cry for me – no, not even one tiny, tichy, tear!

Eating a Julie Mango

Walking Into a London restaurant to buy,
A funny but sorry sight did catch my eye:
A mango dressed as a hedgehog on a plate,
What on earth's changed this mango's fate?

In an instant to back home, I reminisced:
Thinking when young, how very blessed
I was, to savour flavourful *Julie mango* sweet,
While listening to sounds of the Calypso beat.

The sumptuous shape as smooth as silk
Has nectar-filled pulp, like condensed milk,
Brain commands hand with anxious teeth,
Will pierce the fruit, oh so very sweet to eat!

Then reddish-orange, soft, sunset-tinged flesh,
Explodes on tongue, in your mouth, making mess;
Sucking, rotating with so many pleasurable bites,
Teeth scraping the skin; I lick remnants in sight.

Then hands are bathed in sticky, juicy, delight,
Tongue is ready; obliterating all nectar from sight,
Till hard, stony, seed in mouth bruise your teeth,
You suck till you're truly satisfied, in the heat.

Rain

The solo droplet hesitates in mid-air; decides to drizzle, then falls -
With one-two-three; racing in rising crescendo they seem to call,
As they form a rain droplet band, hastily making a watery tune.
They syncopate on roofs, leaves, houses; create an orchestra soon,
Caressing trees, bathing leaves, duo and trio droplets they all sing;
On paper, puddles, cars, caravans and old tin cans – on everything!
Bass reverberates in broken barrels; wet grass, timbrels that ring,
Competing with sopranos from sizzling sounds of vehicles wheels:
These mingle into percussion joined by altos on wet windows sills.
As the dominant cascading torrents lead this rainy instrument band
They multiply; creating myriad mini bands throughout the wet land:
Conducted by the Master on high, they join the sea and then replay;
Repeating an incessant cycle - the rise and fall of a Water Symphony.

A Black Mother to Her Son

That birth day long ago, an angel gifted you to me,
Momentous, precious - a beautiful boy to behold!
Now I watch with the passing of our years and recall
How quickly Time turns days and months into years:
Your handsome face which is maturing with grace
Shows smiling eyes, glowing skin, perfect in your face.

Time as it passes, recalls both of our unfolding years
Your childhood laughter and those funny, petty fears;
Youthfully then, you pretending to be man of the house
To create male role-model when none was around;
Perplexing, you listened and frowned when you learnt
Your dad's not returning, and that it wasn't your fault.

Thumbing through life's pages, scanning our joys and pain
It would be remiss, to fail in my duty to reflect with you
How life as a journey; can be seen as a fast-moving train,
Carrying our ambitions, wishes, wants, goals and desires;
Also on board hate, jealousy, envy, greed, rage and deceit,
Comingled with enemies or schemers; helpers or friends!

Take my advice son, to help steer you in your life's ride,
Be aware of bumps; unplanned stops, some nasty slides
As you look ahead, manoeuvring contours, ruts or bends:
Notice life's controversies that may never seem to end,
Trains in our environment, carry human complex states,
So look for eyes of daggers; and also hearts full of hate.

You must know who you are - no reliance on just Fate;
From racial heritage of kingship, dig deep down; unlearn
Histories and stereotypes, which you must really discern;
In honouring ancestors, don't repeat histories and lies,
But seek knowledge, understanding; reach for the skies
Be clear of your vision, as you work hard for your prize.

Determine to strive beyond the differences and brands;
Innovate, create your own model, it's all in your hands,
You have great strength to bypass glass-ceilings or walls;
Boundaries of colours, genders, and statistics they create.
Unmatched; believe in the power to unlock your potential;
Admirable - but can be used to orchestrate your downfall.

Some things may challenge you, take time to stop and think,
This unpredictable world can push you right over the brink:
Don't settle for less, as God's already chosen you; His best,
Listen to those you love; they too will face life's great tests.
Trust: a word foolishly applied, sources many great pains,
May throw you off-guard; your steadily moving life-train.

Your job is to crack foolish habits, defy fashionable shackles,
So wear trousers in your waist - resist psychological battles;
Dismiss trite trifles; distractions that may legally implicate,
Or activities that pander to stereotypes in actions you take;
Truth is, law-Reps, though not above the law, do obfuscate,
So know your Rights, fight back; your children's life at sake.

Watch every action; ponder each reaction that you make,
As unmistakable education, your children may just imitate;
There'll be moments of happiness, and occasions of pain
When those you love will exit their own life journey train:
But for them and your offspring, you just have to carry on,
Don't wallow in pity, as all journeys must come to an end.

Learn to cherish every moment, and live life to the fullest,
Take every opportunity; strategically, fight for what's good;
For these I have endeavoured and always fervently stood,
Defiantly confident, whilst resolutely, striving as I should,
To assume life's multiple roles; as your mother and father,
Teacher, doctor, protector, psychologist and your friend.

I make no apology for tough moments when I had to scold,
They were intended to steer you through life's path of gold:
Ensure good health, peace, comfort, happiness, and security
In a world full of dangers, strangers and downright misery;
We've laughed, cried, had fun, travelling parts of our world,
Showing you need to be independent, confident, and bold.

Many will wait for your downfall; my dear, NEVER give up!
It's the mantra I leave you, in considering how to redress
Any mishaps, omissions, lapses or just plain forgetfulness:
Life is pulsing moments, embrace it, and follow your dreams,
No room for complacency, the world's not what it seems:
This lesson is simple; have reasons for the things that you do.

Laugh till it hurts you; and son, please don't be afraid to cry;
Not everyone will love you, but for the best you must try,
Find true love; a gift which is not just taking someone's heart
But how much you truly can give, how much you also impart:
For your children's sake, stay very safe; and as you anchor
Them, share your life's story, before your own journey ends.

Falling Down

When we fall down, we must get up!
Whether like a baby taking first steps,
On the ropes of life, or in heavy strife;
    Get back up again!

When we fall down, we must get up!
Whether in a childhood sporting race,
Broken relationship, lost in life's storm;
    Get back up again!

When we fall down, we must get up!
Failed your exams, all kinds of tests,
Business loss, overwhelmed by debts;
    Get back up again!

When we fall down, we must get up!
Forced to change our goals and plans,
Bereaved or carrying hurt and pain;
    Just get back up again!

When we fall down, we must get up!
Disappointed by those whom we trust,
Witness, as enemies plot and scheme;
    Try, just get back up again!

When you fall down, you must get up!
Remember there's one, who judges not,
Unconditional His love; a Healing Balm
That soothes your hurt, cures your pain
    So, get right back up again!

Friday Night - Youth Anthem

Hip! Hip! Hooray!
It's Friday today!
Down tools, quick steps,
Charge home, charge phone,
Short shower, heart beats,
Posse calls, night's planned,
Cheeky clothes, lip glossed,
Perfume spray, hair spray,
Mother's frantic,
Father frowns:
Check - Time back?
Kiss! Mwah! Kiss! Mwah!
Door slams!
S-I-L-E-N-C-E!!
Cool breeze,
Intoxicatingly free
Is this little song-bird;
Who laughs, who shouts,
Who prances and dances
To the Music as it pulses,
Causing bodies to convulse;
Eyes from that corner!
You the teaser, smiles;
That Come on is too fast?
Slow down - that drink!
The night is still young;
Slow down - the pace!
He's now in your face,
'Baby, shake that thing!'
His breath's too close:
Your head in a fuzzy swing,
Mum's voice in your head,
Dad's frown is your dread.
Making a fool of yourself?
There's always next Friday,
And the Friday after that,
Then the next Friday,
And then the next.

Ode to Seasons in the Tropics

Under a bright, cerulean, sun-lit sky
The seasons are wet or crispy dry;
Whether seed time or in harvest
There's time to slow down; to rest -
When wet skies appear to soften
Sun-kissed, tropical plants, in this
Two-seasoned botanical wonderland.

From Rose-mouth and mixed Hibiscus,
To spectacular wild, white Orchids,
Or multi-coloured Bougainvilleas -
Sighing and playing as they tease
Purple, yellow and violet Allamandas:
And the red Jump-up-and-kiss-me
Winks at spidery yellow Aleanders
Infused by airborne aromatic Rose.

Among tree-lined canopy walkways,
Flamboyant, Frangipani and Trumpet trees
Are flanked by towering Palms on high,
Which bathe, when heavy rains cascade
To dance with the flora, of this sunny paradise;
Washing luxurious sun-soaked, thirsty gardens -
Of Jasmine, Jacob's Coat and Desert Rose.
And Birds of Paradise suck the sweet nectar,
While frolicking with Flamingo flowers.

Not for me the wicked, wild, winds of winter,
Nor the crispy, chilly, autumnal breezes,
Or the snow-capped, heated houses;
Surrounded by gardens of powdery, white,
Crunchy snow and freezing, frostbitten, fingers.
These await the sun which, for 6 months has gone,
But will return, to give birth to the coming spring.
No, not for me the glacial snowman, woollen hats or gloves;
That's why I bask in forever summer,
In my two-seasoned botanical wonderland.

Spring

Awaking the earth; spring season brings mirth,
Dressing everything, evidencing nature's birth,
On trees and flowers, birds, animals and bees,
Covering winter's nakedness: our world to please.

She subdues the lingering, cool, winter breezes,
And pleads with sun to increase his degrees;
While Rain rejoices, softening the brown earth,
As multi-coloured attractions all now come forth.

How gently spring winds dance; mildly shakes,
While gardens being mowed will not hesitate
To glow like a prom queen, smile and to show,
That everything in sight, she will surely grow.

Soothing, uplifting, unlatch all doors and wink
At sunlight, fresh blossoms; red, white and pink;
See insects crawl over fresh paths that you make,
Scurrying from their slumber; all now fully awake!

My Grandmother's Hands

I can only imagine her youthful, caring, loving hands,
Soft to touch, tight, oily-glistening, light brown skin;
Showing no creases or ageing or multi-furrowed lines -
Hands which record she prayed, plaited and planted,
Wash, then wrung clothes, whisked, wove and wrote;
Hands which cooked, cleaned, baked bread and bathed,
Or grabbed, grated, grasped, gently rubbed and grew:
Hands that sewed, showed, shelled peas and scolded,
Or clung, clapped, combed hair, caressed and cradled;
All done with love - those small, silky, sun-kissed hands.

But I knew her in later years, with tough matured hands;
Hands that worked hard over three score and ten years,
Witnessed coming and going of our humanity's tears,
The entrance, exit of a lover; changed her into mother,
Then working tirelessly, supplying her grand-kids needs:
How perfect, her fingers; short, stubby, cinnamon colour,
Her left hand ring-finger has a gold ring, among fingers
Tapered by pinkish-white, non-manicured, brittle nails;
And each joint displays soft folds of thick skin creases,
Reveal signs of ageing and a long romance with Time.

Grenville Market

Morning breeze caressed these sun-kissed goods,
Blessed in this Spice Isle our nature's fresh food:
Displayed, a kaleidoscope of multi-coloured hues
Heaped like rainbow pyramids or glistening in trays.
Especially prepared so you can come feast your eyes;
Come by, come and buy; how can you bear to resist?

She stands by her stall, as colourful as her wares,
In hustle-bustle economic splendour - she smiles.
Fill your mouth, feast your eyes, smell the aromas;
Cooked food, fresh fish, and fresh meat to buy:
See star apples, melons, bananas; green or yellow,
Or dare to try mangoes; *Julie*, *Starchie* or *Glenn*
Come - buy some or buy all: she's waiting for you.

See how they are appealing, ripened by His sun,
Sapodillas, sweet potatoes, guineps, and guavas too,
Fig, plantain, bluggoe - in all shapes and all sizes,
Pomerac, golden apples, and crisp governor plums;
Zaboca, French cashew, breadfruit or roasted corn,
Oranges, limes - green, yellowy-green; they're fine,
All bathed in the rain; infused with our island's love.

Tickled by wind, kissed by sun, harvested with care;
Breadfruit, cho-chos, coconuts, gungo peas, and yams,
Paw paws, pineapples, small tanias, stinking-toe too;
Callaloo, dasheen, manioc, pumpkin, roasted cashew,
Look - masala, mace, nutmeg, saffron, and cocoa balls,
Sour-sop, ginger beer, *bois bande*, mauby and sorrel;
Taste them, look, try! You've got to come and buy.

Bright like a picture-book, the splendour of this Isle!
Buy yellow saffron, red mace, our black nutmeg too,
Rough-skin breadfruit, along smooth spinach leaves,
Green zesty cucumbers and our yellow passion fruit,
Brown sapodillas, contrasting red tomatoes, green peas;
Vying for the limelight are fresh, brown hanging crabs,
And beautifully labelled packets; neatly stacked bottles too.

What aesthetic pleasure, a gift of heavenly delight!
Cinnamon spice, cloves, hot sauce; come, you will find
Such a feast for your belly, and a picture for your eyes:
A kaleidoscope of colours; then eat our special *Oil Down*,
It's very, very nice – dare you try; come here and buy!
A visit to Grenada, your next Caribbean holiday spot;
Ask for Market Square, Grenville, in The Isle of Spice.

I Quit!

Fast forward: Success is real, his tempest passed,
A light has come to shine in dark crevices at last,
To ensure end to dangers in the jobless shadows
Restored to workability, refreshed like meadows:
Records were stained; they had blocked his name,
Ensuring he experienced years of no-work shame.

Rewind: He remembers well his loud outburst,
The day when life just got too tough, he cursed
Corporate thugs, he screamed and he hollered;
'I quit! You stole my work for your own gains
And refused to pay for my tireless toil and pains
Slavery - your branded name; it's a public shame!'

Flashback: The chairman's ashen pallor turned dark grey
Before Tribunal judge who made him pay; nothing to say,
But guilty echoes in his mind reverberated, he had to tell
How his Company partners were deliberately misled,
After they realised their contracts were no longer good
Because he'd quit, and no one did their job, as he could.

Now: Will never have to quit, as Chairman of his own
Company; so fairness and justice to his staff are shown:
He recognises each one as an important cog in his wheel
Of fortune, creating wheels of their own; in order to deal
With commitment - families, challenges, stress and strife,
Within strategic goals - to cope with this thing called Life.

I'll Dance at Your Wedding

I'll dance at your wedding,
I'll sing loudly in church,
I'll make merry the moment;
And celebrate the end of your search.

I'll dance at your wedding,
I'll drink champagne on ice,
Happy you've turned out so very nice;
Mature, responsible, with your chosen wife.

I'll dance at your wedding
I'll welcome all your guests
Standing proudly, I'll give you away
Oh can't wait for this most auspicious day.

I'll dance at your wedding
I'll speak power in very few words,
Saying how much I love you,
Reciprocating, how you have cared.

I'll dance at your wedding
Memorise the awesome day,
So when I'm old, frail and grey,
Indelibly, I'll recall and happy to say,
How much I danced and swayed,
On your truly, spectacular, momentous, wedding day.

In the Castle of my Hoodie

My Hoodie – the image-maker, that item of scorn!
Typecasting, it blights my life when it's worn,
Media's playmate mostly used to denigrate:
Or confine me to spaces beyond your jail's gate.
Stereotyped - the source of your innermost fear
Not once, or twice, but 365 days of every year.

Black boy, black man, you - black hoodie dude!
Wearing symbols of threat in the neighbourhood;
On road, and in school, on trains and in your bus,
Seen from behind, expecting black face is a must!
My white friend in his hoodie's not nearly so feared
As when I wear my hoodie; to cover my [1]dreads.

It covers my head, probably saves me from harm,
Soft on my skin, where it's all fuzzy and warm,
My hood keeps me focused on how I want to be,
To choose to see only the things I want to see,
Sporting the colours that your shops rate as "Nice,"
With no fear in your advert, no fear in your price!

Haven't noticed a stigma for your other range of hats:
Scarves, deerstalkers, berets, turbans, bonnets and caps!
You wear them in Derbies, mosques, temples, and church,
But me in expensive hoodie is the man that you search.
Now, safe in my hoodie-castle, is how I want to feel,
Happy in my own clothing: not on your TV newsreel.

Note:
[1]**dreads** – short for dreadlocks – hair worn in Rastafarian style

Island Girl

Her England plan was simple, work 5 years only,
Amass needed funds; then homeward return!
Plump, proud, sleek, smooth-looking, smiling,
Hot-comb straightened hair, gold-teeth looks;
She set sail on the mighty "*Rush*"[1] bound for
The Motherland – 'paved with streets of gold,'
For all her family needs, for their betterment;
So, any job will do.

Cold days, dark nights, no job she could find,
Mouths to feed, plead the missives from home
Raise anxiety, heart throbs but goads her hopes.
Greetings and prayers mixed with island needs:
Medicine for mama's cough; shoes for Jane's feet,
Money to buy books and wood to stop the leaks;
Her action is swift, as solution must be sought;
So, any job will do.

Don't call her lazy, in your *Labour Exchange*,[2]
Her pride – fending for herself; for kith and kin,
Don't sneer at her when the rent's late one day,
She'll take the floor - hire bedroom, just to stay:
Wash dishes today, Firestone factory tomorrow,
Chambermaid at weekend; Sunday's for church,
Yes, strong back, fixed mind, her goal is sure;
So, any job will do.

Incessantly she toiled, she saved; did not stray,
Ambitions set high; get a job, a house, get a car!
The seasons they came - five seasons have flown,
As needs toppled goals, in contests for *Susu hands*[3]
More time must be added – the end not in sight;
Because Life seemed to shatter her England plan,
Testing this patiently planning, proud island girl;
So, any job will do.

Now the years have gone by, she sits and she smiles;
How time has flown fast, turning 5 laboured years to 50!
So she thought of the Queen, and pondered this thought:
Time has been referee to both their joys and their pains,
As they breathed the same air, shared the same years
Witnessing demise - friends, loved ones and Empire too!
Fifty years on, and empire-building, island-girl still works;
But, NOT any job will do!

Note:
1. **"Rush"** – reference being made to HMS Empire Windrush. Empire Windrush was a ship which brought one of first large groups of post-war West Indian immigrants to the United Kingdom in 1948.
2. **Labour Exchange** – the modern version today is the Job Centre Plus. They began in 1909, to help the unemployed find employment
3. **Susu Hands** – an old form of traditional banking among West Indians, where groups of people pool specified sums of money at intervals and donate the total sum collected, in turn, to each member of the group, until each one has the total sum at least once, and then start again.

La Bay

The deep, dark, deceptive, ocean groans and it quivers,
As rising sunlight on its surface glimmers and shimmers;
Beneath it, the ocean god winks at the majesty of the sun
With secret agendas to bless; maybe curse some for fun.
I gaze in awe at the rhythmic rise and its responding fall,
Of waves that lap-talk of beauty, as they crush the wall;
I breathe its salty air and taste the frothy, foaming brine,
As I wonder at its obedience of reaching an invisible line.

Innocent it seems; holds the key to its watery treasure,
From sailors once engaged in commercial adventures,
Deceptively caught in questionable, contentious trade;
As reprimand is heard from spirits in this watery grave;
It is a liquid kingdom of life-giving, limitless sea-food,
Will feed the whole world, so man's life should be good
A medicine chest, with secrets for many global cures -
An encyclopaedia of marine remedies; all should be pure.

It dominates our globe with its vast imposing presence,
Taking earth's 70 and leaving us with only 30 per cent;
Who taught the ocean to keep its watery-blue boundary
From man's structures and our hard surfaced territory?
It speaks to our troubled world of conflict and of strife,
Saying goodbye to the moon; good morning to our lives:
Witnessing the sun's rising in La Bay's tranquil presence,
I'm in awe of its mesmerising beauty and its eerie silence.

Letting Go

She defied the children's [1]PGL school-trip rule,
Turning up at 11 am outside of our school;
Then unsettled the earlier fragile, weepy ones
Who said goodbyes and now expectant of fun.

They filed out in twos, clutching their little bags,
Fully coated and each sporting school name tags;
Excited though hushed, they followed Miss' lead
To wait for the coach that's all they now need.

But mum stood on the opposite pavement
Waving, blowing kisses which were well-meant;
Whilst silently mouthing, "*Love you my darling,*"
Knowing I could get into trouble for calling.

Closer outside my window she stood in the road,
She tapped on the glass and to me she showed,
My battered, one-eyed, and very worn-out Ted,
A sleeping partner, who never ever leaves my bed.

I gasped in surprise and felt quite, quite ashamed,
Of others knowing I still have a teddy with a name!
Embarrassed, I cringed and slid onto the coach floor
And wished I could bolt out the closed Entry door.

My friends, they all laughed, "*You still have a teddy?*"
"*Course not,*" I blushed; my face now a bright cherry;
Secretly I wished the coach would start up and leave,
As my head's in a spin; my stomach's about to heave.

My mind said, "*Go home, mum; stop ruining my street* [2]*cred*;
I no longer want a teddy anywhere near to my bed!"
I did let him go only last night when finally I realized
Boys like me are more grown up and also quite wise.

Glossary: [1]*PGL* is a residential holiday destination for children 7 to 17
[2]*cred* – short for *credibility* or street reputation among friends

Mad Woman: Fact or Fiction?

She defies the odds of imageries fixed,
Castigates you for stereotypical labels
And wilfully tumbles the one in the attic;
Watch, as she flip-sides your own table.

She will play you at your labelling game,
See, this [1]*'mad' woman* is no pushover;
[2]*Anancy* inside her; the trickster spider,
She has many sides you will discover.

Don't say her child's lazy or insolent,
She'll make you recant; or even repent
With noisy behaviour, you'll soon recoil,
When she retorts; *"Just go to hell!"*

The Housing Officer has deprived her,
So has her lazy good-for-nothing lover,
And extended family's disowned her,
Knowing she lost her long-term job;
So, self-esteem is plummeting – low.

The Social Services have questions,
Her sons, they say, are in a pickle;
And don't have a back-home Uncle,
[3]*Tantie, Tata, Nennen,* or close friend
Who'd usually be there to make amends.

She is so burdened with life's trials,
Can hardly deal with the rising strife;
Her head feels like a spinning wheel,
But to stop you all from prying,
You will never ever see her crying!

Truth is she really needs saving now!
So, it is the bank manager's turn:
Refuse help, lessons will be learnt;
So anger bursts: emotions are released!
Don't call for your uniformed security.

She's labelled: an angry, black, woman –
Like the mad woman in the attic
Or some scary monster under cover!
Negotiating parenthood on her own,
Is she really mad or just misunderstood?

---

[1]**See Glossary** – (*"mad woman"*) - for an extended discussion on this

Note:
[2]***Anancy*** is a lead character in Caribbean folktales, who is a hero, but is also a trickster figure, who tried to outwit his Slave Master (during his servile existence on Slave Plantations); operating as an example for others to follow; to avoid punishment and escape from bondage.
[3]***Nennen,*** Caribbean expression for a Godmother
Tantie, Caribbean expression for Auntie
Tata, Caribbean expression for Grandfather

Mum on a City Bus

Three o'clock, Rain! Third bus, no space!
For her double pram there's no empty place
Bus again! Shove! Shout! Crush! Curse!
School children just won't let her get in.

Three-thirty! Still stampede, Push, Rush,
Loud howls, swear words, Banter, Laughter,
Children chatter, Push! Crush! More Shouts!
School children just won't let her get in.

Four o'clock! Her two babes lie in the pram,
So pregnant mum grips her toddler's hand;
Late, but she's finally able to board a bus,
Doors open, less rush, no crush; now no fuss.

Parks pram in the on-bus designated space,
If lucky, she'll find some nearby sitting place
But her fretting toddler refuses to sit still;
Rubbing his tummy; shows where he feels ill.

The babies awake; join in his wailing chorus,
Their mother rocks, coos over pram, then fuss,
But a sitting passenger frets and loudly scolds;
Now she panics - which babe should she hold?

Her ears felt hot, her face went bright red,
The screaming babies just need to be fed;
A full hour late, for their precious dinner time
Because no space on the bus she could find.

Slowly buses accumulate like a winding red snake,
Accident up ahead; Not now, for goodness sake!
Rain, hunger, cries, complaints, fear; stress rise -
As pregnant mum, two babies and toddler cries.

She exits the bus, decides to walk home instead
In the rain: it will help to keep a very cool head,
As she ponders the contesting strains of existing
In this intolerant, impolite, querulous, big city.

My Teacher

My teacher's ass is a pregnant pear,
All Year 9 boys in awe; stop and stare,
Her top so tight, I can't sleep at night
With low-cut, large breasts views in sight.

Mum says our school policy should stop
Teachers who dress in school like sluts:
My friends and I just can't concentrate
With adult flesh displayed on our plates.

Her lessons taught are like sexual tease,
Causes us to do some things just to ease
Our adolescent imaginings running wild;
Though mum says I'm an innocent child.

Only in her class I deliberately act dumb,
Faking I need help, so near she will come
To slowly explain what I already know,
Just to peak at those big breasts on show.

Her Lycra trousers stretch and they cling,
Showing contoured crutch – everything:
And her thick-set legs like trunks of trees -
That body torments us; so stop it please!

Are They Misfits?

The long, long waiting is over at last, he's finally here,
Testing our ability to high-profile plan and to prepare;
Excited with beating hearts, we stood in the long line,
He sauntered in with six securities, looking frail but fine.
In private London chambers we all stood nervously tall,
Talk. Stop. Talk. Along the line, he greets us one and all,
My heart's a beating drum that's threatening with fear.

Legs like jelly shakes, breathing rises, as he comes near.
In quiet subtle tones all our information we did share
As Special Assistant stays close to him – stood very near;
Bending, he listened, information of my students I share,
Head retreating then surprisingly asks; Are they misfits?
What! I don't think it can be anything that I had said,
How stereotypically stupid, strange, surprising to hear!

Her Smile

(Im: Laura Harmsen 1978 – 2012)

When she smiled a thousand dancing little stars would rise,
And circle the vast expanse of the silky, silvery, Milky Way,
Radiating the world like little live sparklers on a firework stick;
This emits yellow sunshine and very bright effervescent rays.
With her head held back, perfect white teeth came into view,
Obeying the stretched soft skin gap, as it invites you and me
To view the world through her happiness and her sweet smile;
Her twinkling small, brown, eyes wink as they are hugged
By laughing lines at the corner of her beautifully shaped eyes.

And amidst her precious and perfectly formed facial symmetry,
Long nose, small eyes, thick eyebrows, soft chin comfortably sits,
Caressed by full head of cascading, long-flowing thick brown hair:
She smiled when she showed her love for others, in true romance,
She smiled that smile of pride and joy resulting from motherhood,
She smiled that smile, which hid life's disappointment and her pain,
She smiled as she hugged you with her last, '*Thanks for everything*',
Laura finally smiled her last smile which said, *"I'll no longer be here,*
    But I leave you something to remember me by," –
Somehow, I think it must have been her smile!

Oh My Soul!

Why are you downcast, Oh my soul?
What is this heaviness within?
My enemies say of me, go perish!
And wait for this time they will cherish.

Why are you downcast, Oh my soul?
What is this fear within?
They whisper ill and trumped-up malice
In slander they bring a poison chalice.

Why are you downcast, Oh my soul?
What is this doubt within?
The wicked hunt my very soul
And falsely push me in a hole.

Why are you downcast, Oh my soul?
What is this pain I feel?
My tears have been my daily food
Though I have lived just to be good.

Why are you downcast, Oh my soul?
What predicts have they planned?
She'll never get up from this place
Let's wipe her out with more disgrace.

What is this voice of peace I hear?
Who speaks to me from within?
Of peace, of love, of faithfulness,
Salvation, mercy and of grace?

In the silence of my broken heart,
I heard a whisper clear; I am your God,
Your Deliverer near, do not ever fear,
Call to me, little child and I will hear.

For days and nights I called and felt
A radiance, joy and strength within;
A ray of hope, a song to sing,
Now I am praising Him, my King.

Old Age Romance

Jane's fallen in love again at the age of 72;
When lovers come calling, what can she do?
Smirking at those who say at this ripe old age,
You are romance-less and stern as an old sage.
Her mind is still intact; her hearts still in place,
Though few wrinkles and lines are on her face;
She wonders, is it possible to keep up the pace?

Sometime last night, she slept with Arthritis,
In brief romance, he infiltrated her left wrist;
Last year Osteoporosis knocked on her door,
But Doctor gave remedy, so he got the elbow;
Two men in Jane's life causes too much strife,
They are excess company for her fragile life.

Cataract, an old lover, no longer comes over,
Was driven away by a surgeon's new lens cover;
And as for Depression, he instantly took flight,
Having learnt her new vision, gave reason to fight:
A battleaxe this Jane, who now rarely complains,
Courageously; she's not accepting any old pain.

Out of the Mouths of Babes...

I watched her innocent 12 year old little face
Become tainted with Death at a very fast pace;
Pouring out watery woes at an alarming rate,
Her mind so clear, innocent; no apparent hate,
Recalled at speed, worries, her inner-most strife;
This evidenced burdens in her little 12year life.
She can't understand when told to *get over it*!

Adult confusion, separation and resenting dad,
Doesn't see why she should label him as bad;
Occasional contacts confirm he is really *cool*,
Whilst mother insists she's no longer his fool:
Until that day when a hospital call intimated,
'Little time left, we heard you were related.'
She can't understand when told to *get over it*!

Too late for preventive mask, apron or gloves,
What she really wants - him alive and his love:
Adult confusion, separation, resentment of dad,
Transformed Mum into trauma, it is so very sad.
If only she had made them hold hands and recall,
That she and her sister will need help if they fall.
She can't understand when told to *get over it*!

Her best friend is bullied, and is also self-harming,
Cos' Adults always arguing, fighting; it's alarming,
While pain was still raw, her grandfather also died,
Then heard a father deliberately took his own life -
From shame in daughter at [1]Uni's disappointment,
Having a boyfriend - cultural taboo that's abhorrent!
She can't understand why she should *get over it*!

How mature she is, still in her Primary school years,
Has suddenly wondered should she continue to bear
The pain and confusion and hell she is now feeling;
Since she blames herself daily, because she is living,
And is wondering if she too, should be self-harming
To block out all the pain: all that she is carrying.
She can't understand why she should *get over it*!

Daily her other friends are encountering the shame,
Repeated bullying and persistent experience of pain:
So as her Class Teacher, Confidant, with great trust,
I know that listening, helping and advising is a must,
To anchor this little life: help her try and negotiate,
The trials and beauty of life she must appreciate.
And to learn that in time; she *WILL get over it*!

Note:
[1] **Uni** – university

Maud's Second Time Around

There's tremor in Maud's legs and arms,
Nothing to do with defiance of her mind:
Walking frame's fixed; focused on her hips,
Her legs await mind's stern instructions -
Forward! But there's no sync, they wobble;
Quick march! Prompts muscles that quiver,
Maud is standing still.

Facial expression, defiance that chastises,
Stiff rebellious legs won't move her frame;
Cold wind blows Maud's long flowing hair,
Covers her eyes, her ears, and her dry mouth -
Grey, is the pallor of her determined face.
Once, she was as good as voices she hears,
Maud is standing still.

Rich, screeching laughter, comingled with
Helter-skelter, running, prancing, hiding -
Catch ya! Silence, by primary recess bell;
Quieter now, another memory propels,
You can do it! Come on honey!
Mother's approval, so toddler acts;
Maud is standing still.

Now in Maud's second time around,
Body won't obey her mind's commands,
It pleads to legs, just one step forward;
First, an inch – success, hip, hooray!
Encouraged by mind, her legs wobble,
Whilst face in recompense, adds a smile,
Maud is now stepping.

The impatient cab driver is clearly very vexed,
Maud's refusal of help; he's no time to spare,
Has duty to perform so he twitches and taps.
Time's not on his side - not as for frail Maud,
 He fails to appreciate her combative mind;
She needs to preserve her determined stance.
 Maud is slowly moving.

 Just like that toddler, he did not hurry,
 Just like that child, he once encouraged,
 Just like that youth, he sent off to school,
 Just like the wilful teenager, he did scold,
 Just like that grandchild he's drooling over:
 Is our Maud, doing her second time around;
 Maud *WILL* keep moving – slowly.

Miracle of Friendship

This miracle of friendship lives in the heart,
You don't how it's appeared or when it starts
But it brings a certain kind of happiness;
Makes you feel unique and really blessed.

Marks your life and like a thread of gold,
Priceless: a gift that can't be bought or sold.
It's a bond that grows even brings romance,
Weathers storms but never fades in distance.

It binds two hearts even when they're apart,
Leaves permanent love footprints in your heart
Lucky we are, when some are sent our way:
How it sometimes bond, we really can't say.

Inspires our joys and shares in our pains,
Whatever the weather; come sunshine or rain,
A true friend will be at your side through it all,
And willing to catch you, whenever you fall.

And like a straight line that never ever bends,
Such love has no boundaries - it never ends:
So when you're apart, it lives in your heart,
There it stays, cemented - just as at the start.

Seasons

He planted his life's goals and watered them well,
Planned his future by investing in houses to sell;
Daily he carefully speculated, nightly he collated,
Pouring over figures; deciding on the risks to take.

Like the coming of spring, there was much at stake.
The years of growth showed more rises than falls,
Were blooming like summer, so friends came to call;
But the fair-weathered ones out-numbered the rest.

As cynosure of gatherings, was a friend to them all,
Who occupied precious moments; his times to reflect.
So his return was a poor harvest that preceded his fall,
As profits plummeted; this he had not time to detect.

Friends happily helped to harvest his stocks and shares;
And braying like donkeys, would grin and compare
His dwindling autumn; with their past, similar, years:
Along came his winter, showing no profits were there.

Too late to realise he had not one remaining share;
Without attention to profits, and increase in his bills,
Banks foreclosed his assets and took away all his keys,
Now *friendly* [1]John Crows are circling; in wait for the kill.

Note:
[1]**John Crow** - A John Crow is a large carrion feeding bird of prey, with a turkey-like, bald, red or black head.

The Storm

I am in a mighty, threatening storm,
Tossed, blown, intentionally thrown;
My fair-weather friends have all flown
So I walk, shrouded by prickly thorns.

The murky waters rise waist-high,
The wind it rages - could almost fly;
Wagging tongues aren't satisfied,
I want to scream, and run and hide.

Though darkness is on every side,
I remember words, recall them all;
When you're afraid, in need, just call,
With such a promise I chose to abide.

So, blow wind blow, you have no might!
Rise waters, rise; rise to any height!
Stop your threats; I know I'm right,
You cannot beat me in this fight!

Lightning flashed as lies were told,
So ancestral banners rose and unfurled;
Thunder clapped and *Ogun* spoke,
'*Who dares to put on you a yoke?*'

[1]*Obatala* and *Legba* made great noises,
Summoning powers in their loud voices;
Yemaya, Oya, Ochosi and *Oshun* came,
Smashing all the betrayers' wilful game.

I watched as they did wield their swords,
As guardians protecting, they all roared,
And forming a mighty invincible shield
Chanted; '*Never, Never,* **NEVER** *yield*!!'

[1]See **Glossary**

Valentine

Don't [1]mamaguy her with your Valentine guise -
Red hearts, chocolates, wine, and red roses too;
Don't smile, grin, or express lying love-words
You pretend; it's what many people try to do,
Time for showing neighbours and fake friends,
How their Valentine's truly this fool's recompense.

Last month you scared her with your hurtful words
That ripped through her heart like a butcher's knife;
Then questioned the meaning, the worth of her life
Through boasts, you retold all your sordid exploits
With others - broke spirit, you wounded her pride;
Five years is quite enough of this sad, hellish life.

She's had her fill, so she's now packed to leave,
Then through crocodile tears, mercy you plead;
Their baby, the bond that's holding her back,
Is innocent as the flower, light pink as a rose,
The only witness to the day you broke her nose
While expressing your love; sorry for the blows!

Last week you wallowed back into the past
Opening painful wounds, so healing can't last;
Stuck in life's mire, you pour water on her fire
Through confused mentality and much brutality:
Now, her life is a volcano; simmering, raging inside,
Ready to spew love's larva; vent the bitterest gall.

Take back the wine you now wantonly pour,
Don't want the steak, nearby knife's all aglow;
Take back the chocolate, it is bitter-sweet now,
Won't look at the red heart, too broken to mend;
She recalls the years, how they still pain her now,
So, don't mamaguy her; fake, futile is your Valentine!

Note:[1].**Mamaguy** - to deceive or tease someone either as a joke or with fake flattery.

What About Us?

Righting the wrongs of history's deceptive past,
To set the record straight for present kids at last.
But it can lead us all into a box of Pandora's mess,
Though the lessons learnt were meant to redress.

In school assembly, our teachers were very proud,
Their slide shows present things we had not heard
About the past black and white historic dichotomy,
And lots of facts that were not really about me!

In Shire schools our white-washed education
Did complicate Black History month's passion;
Showed us education's deliberate misapplication,
So the penny dropped and made me question.

What about brown between black and white?
History is still lacking; more facts to put right,
It seems to always repeat, so what of our plight?
And from which historic platform do we fight?

Woman of Destiny!
(Ode to the Sisters)

You are a Woman of Destiny!
A child of our created universe,
Uniquely fashioned by loving hands;
Invested with great strength, born to shine,
An oracle of our culture's transmission:
Friend of the parentless, daughter of nations,
Defiantly confident, misunderstood; yet resolute!
Humble before God and loving to all –
You, Woman of Destiny!

Uniquely charactered with purpose and vision,
Though trials assail you, you never can fall!
Daily you smile and honour your Creator –
Today, I am a Woman of Destiny!
With you, no one can compare;
Try her resolve, if you dare!
Anointed to teach, preach and reach
Generations long predestined in the Master's plan;
Yes, you are a Woman of Destiny!

Targeted by enemies, assassins may trail,
But a Woman of Destiny can never ever fail!
Hail princess of the universe! Hail daughter of Zion!
There's nothing you can't do, with strength from God.
Walk in Victory! And yes, Walk tall!
Fear nothing and Never ever give up!
You can do all things, 'Cos you know who you are,
A jewel in the centre of the Master's crown:
What manner of creation is she? Don't you know?
A Woman of Destiny; that's you – that's me!

Down, But Not Out!

Under attack! Targeted! Scupper! See them run!
Rat-tat-tat! Dodging bullets, bombs and big guns,
Blasting bloody bodies with death panic and fear
Sweating; he awoke from old recurring nightmare.

Veteran, patriotic, a soldier when he was needed,
Mind shattered, body battered; once he did lead,
So that's why no one has the right, at him to shout -
Calling him dirty, detestable; a smelly down and out!

His war is not over now in his re-enacting field,
As therapies just can't cure, how haunted he feels,
So he swaps comfy quarters for sleeping outside
Looking for solace - a space for his mind to hide.

Emaciated frame, no food, what a terrible shame!
Passing, you scorn him as if born with no name,
To you he's dirty; a destitute who is now down,
But on this veteran soldier, never ever frown!

Kaiso Farewell Rhythms!

(In memory of Lord Superior, Mighty Composer, Shadow, and DeFosto - 2018)

Farewell, Shadow!
Fare thee well, Mighty Composer
So long, our beloved DeFosto;
Bye, Bye, Lord Superior,
All gone to a distant land,
Into the great Night Shift
There you will sing,
Sing your songs,
Whine you waist,
Tell it like it was.
Sing when you meet the rest
Sing extempore again!
Sing to your heart's content,
Kaiso! for breakfast, Kaiso!
Lunch, dinner, Kaiso for tea!
We know you will sing,
Sing your songs,
Whine you waist,
Tell it like it was.
We wish that we could see you now,
Striking up noisy bacchanals
Making, sweet, sweet melodies,
Taking full control of Kaiso bands
In the land beyond our skies
Where you will sing,
Sing your songs,
Whine you waist,
Tell it like it was.

No time for singing sad refrains,
No crying farewells, not from us,
We focus not on sorrow now
But your undisputed 'people's voice,'
The joy and knowledge you did share
Will influence our youth right here;
So they'll emulate you as they
    Sing your songs,
        Whine their waist,
            Tell it like it is.
Etched forever in our hearts,
So all parting pains must depart,
And in this bitter-sweet farewell
We salute you all and won't relent
From keeping your Kaiso strong!
    As we sing your songs
        Whine we waist,
            Tell it like you did.
So long, our Kaiso giants of old!
Past Leaders of our nation's flock
Griots you were, without any fear,
    Yes, [1]Shikamoo!
    So long! Bye, Bye!
    Fare – thee - well.
    Keep singing your songs,
        Whining your waist,
            And tell it like it is.

Note: [1].Shikamoo – A Swahili word meaning, **"*I respect you.*"**

A Tribute to Calypsonians who passed away in 2018
Mighty Composer (Fred Mitchell); 1935-2018 - 83 yrs
DeFosto "The Original DeFosto Himself," (Winston Scarborough); 1954-2018 – 64 yrs
Lord Superior (Dr. Andrew Marcano); 1937-2018 – 76yrs
The Mighty Shadow (Winston Anthony Bailey); 1941-2018 – 77yrs.

Equality

Expectantly they came and sat down one by one,
To the hospital seats provided they were all shown;
On benches, on chairs, in large white-washed room
Hoping to be relieved and seen by the Doctor soon.
Some limping, clutching, bending and shuffling too,
Others aching, sneezing, wincing, wet eyes weeping;
But the UN couldn't be more globally represented,
As man, boy, woman with babe, and builder relent
Their woeful conditions; from GPs they were sent.

That 25 year old girl with burns winces and sighs,
Holds her waist and left hip, and limps as she cries;
A haggard husband around 60, walks bent due to pain,
So he shuffles, and sweats, writhing with facial strain.
Nurses serve painkillers with hopeful smiles to ease;
Reassuring, they administer saline solutions on wheels.
Someone rushes; a dad overcome with unbearable pain -
This man could barely answer, even to his own name,
As Anxiety walked pompously with Fear; see them reign!

Hope showed on some faces despite all feeling the same,
In room full of sickness, panic, worry, pain and real strain
Who said the world has hierarchy or even stereotypes?
Who here's got more money; who is rich, black, or white?
You can't tell who lives in flat, house, studio or tall tower;
Does Pain or Sickness show respect to those with power?
This room is an echoing chamber, full of painful feelings
Minds that can't think straight; bodies needing healing;
Let's hear it for Pain-the-Equalizer; who levels all status
So now you can see, there really **is** equality, after all!

Conversations in Rhythms

He said,	She said,
Let there be!	Let's have a baby!
So for you and me	So you and me
He planted trees,	Can start a beautiful family
Then commanded the sea	And grow a love child of our own.
of waters very deep, to wait	So in the spring, their time of growth,
At boundary they forever meet	She gave him soil, he planted seeds,
The Land, whilst lapping at your feet.	She ate for two, then grew and grew;
So bright the light and fast He made,	With doctor scan, the sex they knew
To contrast night when the day fades;	A boy is coming; there is so much joy!
The seasons come with burst of spring,	Not long, and off to school he was sent,
As loudly, everything in nature sings:	Their years of summer were soon spent,
All meadows, mountains, hills show life,	As time in his season flew and so he grew,
As variegated plants and animals strive,	Like summer's healthy blooms of flowers
Birds, flowers, fish, and wild honey bees;	With full strength and intellectual powers;
Witness babbling brooks running to the sea	His University days ends with proud degree
Hark! I hear nature sounds in symphony -	Competitive; and most confident to see.
An incomparable orchestral harmony.	Then not long he won a maiden's heart,
The earth so fully blessed is shown,	Pledging; they vowed to never part.
When food and fruits are fully grown;	In their autumn days she was his wife
From rain and sun and then some more	And children gave them a happy life.
And soon there is harvest; grains to store.	They planned for future years ahead,
For times of dryness are awaited; ahead	When growing old will show increase in age:
When winter dark days force us to rest,	Time that reflects life coming to winter stage,
In rhythms showing He knows best.	Must put all physical strength to the test.
So all - in land, in sea and in air, must	So memory recalls their rhythms in life,
Move in His rhythms without any fear.	As they await His final season with no strife,
For winter comes as death and sleeps	When stealthily death comes as winter asleep,
In the cyclic seasons, we're made to keep.	In cyclical life-rhythms that they must keep.

I Will Keep Rising

I will keep rising, like the sun at each dawn,
Singing merry tunes whilst writing my words,
Like the moon that could never stop to rest,
But just goes spinning round our circular earth.

I will continue to dismiss grief and its silly show,
To prove it can never hijack the joys that I know,
Or break this soft heart of unquenchable mirth;
That's mapped with infallible destiny from birth.

I will continue to climb hills, stand on mountains,
Perhaps only stopping to peek at the vast plains,
Passing all birds and those fallen flowers as I rise;
And from high, I'll wonder at the earth and skies.

I will continue with long dedicated affirmations,
Wearing big smiles; making serious declarations,
Confidently knowing there is no scar or a hole,
In this soaring, rising, indomitable, happy soul.

I will keep wearing soft ringlets in my black hair,
And daily still put make-up on my face with care
Till out of sight, beyond the moon, sun and skies;
I will keep rising, and inspire you too, as you rise.

National Mentality

Oh century full of confusing contradictions
In life; with many long-held existential questions!
Is your brain still sliced by [1]British Imperialisation?
Or confused, calculates in repeated metrification?
What's the state of your national mentality?

Did your past education drilled imperial vernacular,
So your height's tall; not short in metric measure?
Do you refuse the habits set in another jurisdiction?
Or, have you baked in kilos and weighed in pounds;
Bought a pint of milk; confusedly, drank it in litres?

Was your strawberry eaten in grams, or converted
To ounces, when mind forgot how to metric weigh?
And the football match played in France, did not
Confuse you, when the ball was kicked at 50 yards;
Now wonder if you should buy your petrol in gallons.

Last week, this was upstaged by geopolitical position,
When a US Cook Show Host measured food in cupfuls;
So my hard-wired mind says it's really no longer logical
To accept your recommended metric's predominance,
Despite facts that the government [2]metrified our lives.

So, today I woke up in a strange and ambivalent mood,
And made my cup of tea with imperial measured water,
My bed-clothes and sheets, in yards I carefully folded,
Ate breakfast eggs, which no longer has a metric taste,
With my toasted bread; smeared in an ounce of butter!

Resistant - lifetime habits simply just don't switch over,
From my yards and miles, to your kilometres or metres:
No personal mandate to change the habits that stuck
In transition; so my brain says, just do as you please!
So, what's the state of your national mentality?

[1] .British Imperial Measurements & [2] Metric Measurement - **See Glossary**

Dancing with Stars

I danced with you and the stars in my sleep,
Catapulting over cotton-cloud shapes as we meet,
Colliding into bouncy dreams as I sing of our love -
A love-song meant to stir your un-beating heart,
Pretending - thinking and wishing we did not part.

I danced and pranced and saw in my mind's eye
The pictures of you on the night that we met,
And waited for twinkles in eyes that have faded
So mine watered, waiting; as in yours I just gazed,
Then leapt and bounced in the air without care.

I chased the storm clouds that caused so much fear,
When I listened to beating heart, disease that's rare,
Pleading with doctors who couldn't cure what's there.
So now I'm dancing with you and the stars in my sleep,
Knowing when I'm fully awake, you will not be near.

Diaspora Blues

He had not considered the real-life consequences
Of leaving home, travelling without family defences;
But tight ties that remain, kept contact phone calls,
Creating confusion and stress in a foreigner's land.
Persistent payment of remittance which is a must,
Tips financial balance, causing near economic bust:
Worry plunges him in fear of joblessness and panic,
Threatening; no time to commit to advancement
To exit his cycle of stress, strain or even the mess,
And alleviate his situation to make some redress.
In environment where *multi* is king of existence,
It causes problems for his *mono* cultural ideology,
So he wallows in isolation and masculine restraint,
Pretending as man; he could deal with all the pain.

Won't off-load his burdens, so in pity he remains,
Pining for communal practice of problems to share,
But the gossip and reproach are his real life scares.
Though he must send materials and money to buy
Things for home, it becomes a regrettable sacrifice.
So to bypass his strict religious rules and prying eyes,
He breaks tabooed practices at night to overcome
Physical needs: the loneliness that his culture forbids.
So puts on a brave face, shows photos when he talks
Concealing his back pain that affects how he now walks.
He masks the reality of struggling to raise more money
For dependent family at home, and his country's GDP;
So hides behind faces; deceiving the woman he keeps
At home: from foreign women with whom he sleeps.

Note:
Diaspora is the movement, migration, or scattering of a people away from their established or ancestral homeland.

Who is he?

There never was one so loathed, so utterly vilified
  In all the earth, so feared, despised or talked about
    With conspiracies to erase him, epidemically rife!

Fear and terror he strikes in most people's heart
  Causing them to grovel, beg right from the start
    Especially when life doesn't go as they plan.

Vocally, some have threatened and needed to kill
  While others fear his presence when he is near,
    But in his absence may plead for him with tears.

He may laugh and jeer with a wicked, sinister, cackle
  When visiting the end of your own life cycle;
    So losing his fight, some will scream, also shout.

In birth-rooms, places where he is quite hated,
  Is cursed for his lingering, especially by the ill-fated,
    While for others, he is really much appreciated.

Many abuse him; hate, when being exam-tested
  But in a fire rescue, runs your Brigade to shield,
    While speed controls in Ambulance to him yield.

You need him, when your life hangs in the balance,
  Or slowly, he will play, with your last fighting chance;
    And terrify your loved ones with over-riding might.

He's impossible to beat or to really fight against,
  Because infused in your life: he's an invaluable host
    Whose name is TIME: the one we need the most!

I aint no snitch!

Sometimes it's hard to say things that need to be said,
When a social tidal wave is rumbling inside your head;
Street threats, parents trust; bodies end up in the dust,
And blood stains the landscape as wolfish media lusts.
      It's a survival game to hide the pain,
      'Cos I aint no snitch; this life is a bitch!

Declan swapped his knife, they say, for 42"calibre gun,
Because his arch-enemy, Tyrone, has gone on the run;
Who you complain to, dodging silent gun or the knife?
Knowing if you talk, it's the end of family or your life.
      It's a survival game to hide the pain,
      'Cos I aint no snitch; this life is a bitch!

Mum took us to church, Pastor preached against crimes,
I tremble inside, knowing his next funeral could be mine;
So Mr. Richer, our teacher, called in a weapons' amnesty,
But how could I hand in mine; I could get cut like a pasty?
      It's a survival game to hide the pain,
      'Cos I aint no snitch; this life is a bitch!

The street is a battlefield with lots of alleyway-trenches,
Hidden stairwells, parks, malls, even sitting on benches!
The worlds where enemies attack are subtle and silent,
Hard to detect the very bullet to you that may be sent;
      It's a survival game to hide the pain.
      'Cos I aint no snitch; this life is a bitch!

But Jason, my 13yr younger brother, Jake killed last night,
Stabbed, going home alone from school; knifed on his bike.
My mum's heart a bleeding coffin; her baby they've slain,
I'm forced to weapon-talk now; as there's nothing to hide
No resurrection - so I'm nursing my much wounded pride,
      Still, I aint no snitch; 'cos this life is a bitch!

It's too late for Brother Jason, but not too late for killer-Jake,
Who'll have to face hate as we wait, in or outside of his jail:
And for my dead innocent, brother, we openly cry; we wail,
Knowing word on the street is, Jake's death has been trailed
So now someone else's name is linked to the murder chain;
      It's a survival game to hide the pain,
      I'm no snitch! This life - It's just a real bitch!

Note:
A *Snitch* is an informant, such as a person who tells the authority (e.g. a police, teacher); about something wrong that a person has done. This is regarded as leading to damaging, dangerous and death consequences.

Goodbye!

There's nothing good about the word goodbye
It's a parting, separation, for now or forever;
Final, in some personally expressed sentiments,
Temporary, it has see-you-later compliments.

Who knows, but you, what a goodbye means?
Perhaps it's that we're not together now, it seems.

A certain goodbye can sever over-bearing ties of old,
Or signpost memories that you must put on hold,
The parting tones expressed, pretty much says it all,
I've had enough of you, so it's our last damn call!

The business deal sealed in firm goodbye handshake,
Or emotional distance, goodbye may show we'll wait;
Love's first goodbye lingers, hesitates - an ugly word,
Or in last embrace; nothing from me will be heard.
But why not tell me goodbye with words that makes more sense?
Cheerio!
Tara,
Toodle-oo!
So long!
Bye-bye!
Farewell!
See you later!
God speed!
Ah gone!
Walk Good!
Me soon come!
Later!
Safe!
I don't think I'll have to ask you what these goodbyes mean.

GLOSSARY

Ivan's War

1. **Hurricane Janet** was the most powerful tropical cyclone of the 1955 Atlantic hurricane season and one of the strongest Atlantic hurricanes on record with wind speeds up to175 mph. Janet was also the first named storm to have 1,000 deaths as well as the first Category 5 named storm to be retired. Hurricane Janet passed between the islands of Grenada and Carriacou in the early hours of September 23, killing 500 people in the Caribbean area. All bridges in Grenada's interior regions collapsed, and spice crops sustained heavy damage. An estimated 75% of nutmeg plantations were destroyed along with nearly all of the island's banana and cocoa crops. Over $2.8 million in damages were estimated throughout the Grenadines.

2. **Hurricane Ivan** - On September 7, 2004, Hurricane Ivan, a category 3 storm, struck the Caribbean island of Grenada, causing widespread destruction. The financial cost of the disaster was estimated at more than US$900 million, more than twice the country's GDP. The hurricane damaged more than 80 percent of the country's building structures, and only two of the 75 public schools remained undamaged. The hurricane damaged more than 14,000 homes and destroyed 30% of the houses, leaving about 18,000 people homeless. A total of 39 people were killed by the hurricane on the island. Some hurricane information sources put the winds from Hurricane Ivan near 130 mph (210 km/h). Severe disruption of the health sector also occurred, including the almost complete destruction of Princess Alice, the island's second largest hospital. An estimated 80 percent of the power distribution grid was lost, and nearly 70 percent of the tourism infrastructure was rendered uninhabitable. Hurricane Ivan also badly damaged the agricultural sector, with widespread damage to nutmeg crops, the island's principal agricultural export. (**Source:** *"Report from World Bank – 23.09.2009).*

3. An **armistice** is an agreement between countries that are at war with one another to stop. The word has two Greek roots: *arma* which means "weapons," and *stitium* which means "stoppage." Therefore when armistice is used, it is a sign that both sides want to give peace a chance; as a temporary battle time-out. The word "armistice" is relevant here as hurricanes are seasonal in the tropical region; meaning, there is a sense of a break or truce, until the next hurricane arrives sometime in the future.

London

The West India Regiments (WIR) were infantry units of the British Army recruited from and normally stationed in the British colonies of the Caribbean between 1795 and 1927. In 1888 there were two West India Regiments in existence, and in 1915 The British War Office decided to group them together into a single regiment, named the British West Indies Regiment. This regiment differed from similar forces which were formed in other parts of the British Empire; meaning they were an integral part of the regular British Army. A total of 15,600 men of the British West Indies Regiment served with the Allied forces. Jamaica contributed two-thirds of these volunteers, while others came from Trinidad and Tobago, Barbados, the Bahamas, British Honduras, Grenada, British Guiana (now Guyana), the Leeward Islands, St Lucia and St Vincent.

Ode to the Thames

1. **Guy Fawkes** - On 5th November, 1605, a York man called Guy Fawkes, also known as Guido Fawkes, with others, planned to assassinate King James 1 and restore the throne to a Catholic monarch. They hired a cellar under the Houses of Parliament, and Fawkes was placed in charge of the 36 barrels of gunpowder which they had smuggled and stock piled there. But their plan was foiled when someone tipped the authorities in an anonymous letter, prompting them to search Westminster Palace. During the early hours of 5th November, they found Guy Fawkes guarding the explosives. He was questioned and tortured over days after which he confessed. Then in January 1605, he was put to death in Westminster by hanging, drawing and quartering. His remains were distributed around the 4 corners of the UK as a stark warning to would-be plotters.

2. **Marchioness** - In the early hours of 20 August 1989, the pleasure steamer Marchioness sank after being hit twice by the dredger Bowbelle at about 1:46 am; between Cannon Street Railway Bridge and Southwark Bridge. The Marchioness collided with the barge, which hit it about its centre, then mounted it, pushing it under the water like a toy boat. Within a matter of about 20 seconds Marchioness had totally disappeared underneath the water. From the 130 people on board Marchioness, 79 survived and 51 died the deaths of 51 people.

3. **New** - meaning annual New Year Celebrations - Each year you can see the spectacular New Years fireworks from the River Thames. It is most sought after as a magical place to be to ring in the New Year.

National Mentality
1. **British Imperial Measurements** - The British Imperial System of imperial units was the traditional system of weights and measures that were used officially in Britain from 1824, by the British Weights and Measures Act. This was overtaken when Britain adopted the metric system in 1965. That is why British Imperial units are now legally defined in metric terms. Interestingly, while the British were reforming their weights and measures in the 19th century, the Americans were just beginning to adopt units based on those were discarding in the 1924 Act!

Brexit
1. In 2012, the blend of the word British (or Britain) and exit, making Brexit, was coined to mean the withdrawal of the United Kingdom from the European Union.

Ode to Seasons in the Tropics
1. An *Ode* is a kind of poem devoted to the praise of a person, animal, or thing.

Letting Go
1. **PGL** is a residential holiday destination for children 7 to 17, which offers a summer-camp type of multi-activity break, away from parents, with activities that allow children the freedom to express themselves in a safe and supportive environment.
2. *Cred.* short for credibility or street reputation among friends

The Storm

1. Ogun, Obatala, Legba, Yemaya, Oya, Ochosi, and Oshun are known as the 7 African Powers. The 7 African Powers are seven of the most well- known and celebrated deities (orishas) of the Yoruban pantheon.

Mad Woman: Fact or Fiction?

The phrase *"the mad woman,"* in this poem, alludes to Charlotte Bronte's character, Bertha Mason, (in *Jane Eyre*); Rochester's insane wife, who is a Jamaican of mixed race, and locked in the attic of his house with Grace Poole as her nursemaid. Such connotations of *madness*, a perception of the exotic female character during the Victorian period, also represents an intense power of sexually , yet at the same time, there is also a deceptive smartness and ruthlessness in Bertha's make-up; since she chose to commit suicide.

According to Sandra Gilbert and Susan Gubar *"The Mad Woman in the Attic"* (1979); all female characters in male-authored books of that time, projected the female as either an *"angel"* or a *"monster."* However, Bertha's position is also part of a larger, social question of femininity and *"otherness,"* in a male-dominated society that characterised the female as having sensual, passionate but rebellious and uncontrollable qualities. This perception caused a good deal of anxiety among Victorian men of that period.

However, alluding to the reference of the *"mad woman in the attic"* in this poem also highlights a stereotype, that the black female is always seen as *aggressive* or *mad*, in her day-to-day interactions with officials and those in authority. This poem, **Mad Woman: Fact or Fiction**, shows the female as refusing to be in a position of inferiority, but at the same time, making use of society's folly of the *labelling principle*, much to her advantage. She panders, like *Anancy* the trickster figure, to the stereotypes of both *"angel"* and *"monster,"* with reference to social expectations; showing much of the anger that characterises the *"monster,"* whilst at the same time, displaying characteristics of the *"angel,"* in embracing the pain of one-parenthood, being protective, refusing to be submissive, and overall is also the defined character of a mother, in an unsupportive social and domestic environment. In other words, she can be labelled as insane, ruthless, socially isolated or discriminated against, but she still emits a power that makes her seem invincible.

Here are some students' analytical responses to the poem, *Island Girl*, by Roselle Thompson, done as UNSEEN POETRY; in preparation for their English GCSE exam.

TASK: *How has the poet presented the theme of migrant struggles in Island Girl?* (Version 1)

> The poet has presented the theme of migrant struggle in the poem "*Island Girl*" through the hardship of caring for a family on a low budget. The poetic voice needs "medicine for mama's cough; shoes for Jane's feet. Money to buy books...so any job will do". The asyndetic listing emphasises the urgency of her situation as is the single line, ending the stanza "so any job will do;" which suggests that the speaker is desperate for money.
> This contrasts with the situation that people born of that country go through, as they are presented with time to spare, whereas she is presented with an opportunity to grasp within a given time. Also what would strike the reader would be that the fact that the poetic voice is working for basic necessities; hence evoking the feeling of sympathy. This struggle of caring for others is mirrored in stanza 3, where she is, "fending for herself" and "for kith and for kin". The collective nouns, "kith and kin" juxtapose the pronoun "herself," and present the difference in what she is doing to help her family and what they are doing to help her. This also emphasises the fact that the poetic voice is a singular person; metaphorically carrying their family on their back which again, contrasts to the situation of a person born in that country; who would have their family, metaphorically caring them. This may make the reader wonder why a society is able to be extremely different within the same country.
> The poet also presents the theme of migrant struggles through the sequencing of the stanzas in the poem "*Island Girl*". The poem is split into 5 stanzas, representing the "5 years only" work placement that the speaker was originally aiming for.
> However, as the poem progresses, stanzas 2 and 3 are filled with hectic asyndetic listing, reflecting upon how the "island Girl" is starting off her life in this new country, which is full of "raised" anxiety and "hiring a bedroom", just to stay. This represents the rational fear of starting something new which could be related to the reader and a young audience, however, could also be unrelatable, as this can be a struggle that comes with being a migrant in an unfamiliar territory.
> However, there is a Volta as the time changes; leading up to stanza 4; which also mirrors the unexpected changes that life can throw at you. "Incessantly she toiled, she saved; did not stray".

This tone of ambition from the adverb "incessantly" suggests that she had to keep trying, though there must have been drawbacks that were holding her down at times; hence, also proving that migrants are tough people who have also tackled a lot of issues in their lives. This can be seen as inspirational to the reader, as moving to an unfamiliar country is draining but being also able to keep up with the challenges there, can be seen as an act of true resilience.

The poet also presents the theme of migrant struggle in the poem "*Island Girl*", through the contrast between what's expected and what's given. The speaker was originally going to, "work [for] 5 years only...then homeward return." However the expected, "5 laboured years [turned] to 50!" The contrast of the uses of exclamation marks used in the first stanza and the last stanza, show the progression of how life works. The exclamation mark in the first stanza represents excitement, whereas the exclamation mark in stanza 5 represents disbelief. (By: *Dinishya: Age 15years*)

TASK: *How has the poet presented the theme of migrant struggles in Island Girl?* - (Version 2)

The poet has presented the theme of migrant struggle in the poem *Island Girl*, through the way she has been presented as willing to do anything to make a better life for herself. This is seen through the repetition of "so any job will do" throughout the poem. This emphasises the fact that she is willing to do whatever she has to, in order to survive and earn money. This is reiterated when it says that she is "washing dishes today, Firestone factory tomorrow, Chambermaid at weekends". The tri-colon shows all the jobs she is willing to undertake. It also makes the work seem endless, as if she is constantly working with no stop. Furthermore, the poem is written in free verse, and has five eight-line stanzas. It could have been written like this to make it seem endless, no matter what she does. This shows the migrant struggle as having to be constantly working to survive and the jobs that she is doing are not the best. Furthermore, it would probably seem quite unpleasant to a contemporary reader, which further emphasises the struggles they have to go through as if her life is not going to change.

The poet has also presented the theme of migrant struggle in this poem by showing all the things that she has to take care of. This is seen when she says she needs "medicines for mama's cough; shoes for Jane's feet, Money to buy books and wood to stop the leaks."

The asyndetic listing makes it all seem endless, as if the problems will never stop. It makes it seem as if the moment she solves one problem, then more will take its place. Her struggle is shown when she tries to solve the problems which is seen when it says, "incessantly she toiled, she saved." The adverb "incessantly" emphasises the fact that she is constantly working, without stopping and makes it sound almost burdensome, with no joy in it; emphasising her struggle to earn enough money to make ends meet and to help her family.

The poet has also presented the theme of migrant struggle in this poem through her initial plan when coming to England in the first stanza; compared to the harsh reality of it in the last stanza. This is seen in the first stanza when it says "her England plan was simple – work 5 years only". The adjective "only" almost suggests her naivety, because she believed that it would be easy, which contrasts with stanza 5 when it says, "turned 5 laboured years to 50". The huge contrast in the two numbers emphasises the fact that she was wrong in her initial beliefs and shows that she thought it would be easy. However, the change in the last stanza to "but NOT any job will do!" emphasises the fact that her ideals and goals have changed, and she has realised through her struggles, that life is much harder than she thought it would be. The capitalized emphatic "NOT" also shows how she has changed and grown with her struggles. **(By: *Oshini* Age: 15 years)**

TASK: Discuss *how the Theme of Nature is presented in these two poems; "Ivan's War" and "Spring" By Roselle Thompson?*

Both poems present the theme of nature but in opposing ways, unlike their formats which are similar. The poem *Spring* is a ballad that introduces the season of spring as newly emerging. The use of the feminine voice, in order to present this is effective, as it allows the reader to grasp the beauty of nature as it is newly birthing life in spring. Firstly, spring is presented through the semantic field of nature itself, and is evident in the first quatrain by the listing "flowers, birds, animals and bees". Nature is then further developed as just beginning in the third quatrain, where "spring winds" are personified as "gently dancing." The use of this adverb is effective, as it crafts a tranquil mood and an atmosphere full of awe. Additionally, the adverb connotes carefulness. This followed by the verb "dance" is what builds this atmosphere of awe, as the reader becomes engaged due to the description of the wind "dancing". Then there is a shift in focus to the garden, which is described by a simile to, "glow like a prom queen".

The verb "glow" has connotations of light and innocence and the noun "queen" connotes power. This therefore alludes to the powerful and astounding beauty spring brings when it comes. Furthermore, the extensive use of the AABB rhyme scheme is effective; delivering and allowing the reader to feel the awe the writer feels about spring. This awe towards nature is further accentuated by the repeated use of triplets; "soothing uplifting, unlatch" and "red, white and pink". The triplets are successful in crafting an image in the reader, of bright intimate colours that have a calming effect when seen. So nature is presented here as beauty that has a tranquil effect when viewed.

In contrast to the *Spring* poem, Thompson presents nature in five quatrains, with violent imagery. This is clear, in *Ivan's War*, as it describes Hurricane Ivan as being at "war," which is mentioned in the title of the poem. It has connotations of death and destruction. This violence of nature is then conveyed throughout the poem and is prominent in the fixed rhyme scheme that has a violent tone. For example, the harsh sounds of "s" in the rhyming couplet "aghast" and "blast" is effective in bringing out this chaotic imagery. This, followed by the simile, "like spitfire blasts," is effective in solidifying this disastrous image of the hurricane because it crafts auditory image of the sounds; whilst the noun "spitfire," presents the military imagery of bombing as in a war.

The power of the hurricane is presented as able to "clobbered the strong trees". The aggressive verb "clobbered" presents a violent tone, due to the sound of the double "bb" consonants, as well as the fact that it is able to bring down "strong trees" conveys its power. This power is further expressed through another simile "for hours he spewed rain like a savage wild beast". The adjectives "savage" and "wild" connote zoomorphic imagery of an animal with actions that lack remorse or sympathy; therefore illustrating the devastation and the violence of nature. This violence and destruction is further enforced in the poem through the use of caesura. The caesura is effective here, as it disrupts the flow, therefore bringing out a disrupted violent image like the "spitfire blast" mentioned in the first quatrain. Therefore, the poet presents nature in *Ivan's War* as violent. Overall, as far as the two poems are concerned, Thompson presents nature as both beautiful and tranquil, as seen in *Spring* but violent and destructive in *Ivan's War*.
(By: *Sankari: Age 15years*)

www.ingramcontent.com/pod-product-compliance
Lightning Source LLC
Chambersburg PA
CBHW050605300426
44112CB00013B/2076